Don Fishback

OPTIONS FOR BEGINNERS

Table of Contents

Don Fishback

OPTIONS FOR BEGINNERS

You *Can* Beat The Market, If You Control The Rules

It's shocking but true. Making money trading can be incredibly difficult. Investment gurus will tell you that you have to be invested in the stock market to truly strike it rich. But that sure doesn't protect you from declining markets.

And if you want a *safe* investment, you sure aren't going to find much inflation protection from a bank account paying 4%.

The only true way to make a decent return and stay protected when the market heads lower is to trade. But based on the performance of most money managers, even that is extraordinarily difficult.

Ironically, trading boils down to just one simple rule: Buy low and sell high. It doesn't matter whether you're trading stocks, mutual funds, real estate, collectibles, or futures or options. It's just that simple.

While the concept is simple, the *implementation* has confounded novice investors, academics and professional traders since the beginning of organized financial markets. That's because no one has been able to accurately figure out how high is high, and how low is low.

Sure, we've all seen and heard about those who have beaten the market for *brief* periods at a time. But none of them, except for maybe a handful, beat the market for *extended* periods. There are numerous studies showing that investors would be far better off simply investing in a basket of stocks mimicking a stock index, and then doing nothing, instead of placing money with a professional money manager.

This shouldn't come as a major surprise. One look at the quarterly mutual fund statistics is evidence enough that even the pros, with, collectively, billions of dollars in financial market research at their disposal, cannot beat the major market averages. It is a sad fact that over the long haul, about 70% to 80% of all money managers fail to beat the market. In other words, only 20% to 30% of all market professionals actually earn their management fee.

As if that 20% to 30% figure wasn't bad enough, unfortunately, it's actually a lot worse. That's because the 20% to 30% that beat the market one year usually aren't the same 20% to 30% that beat the market the next year. In other words, if you happened to have placed money with a pro who was a top performer in 1997, there is a high probability that your money manager will underperform the market in 1998. This rotational aspect to managers means that, over a five year span, the probability that a money manager will beat the market during the entire five year span is less than 1/10th of one percent!

With so many people, many of them with millions of dollars in research resources, trying to beat the market, and only a select few actually achieving their objective, that should tell you how difficult buying low and selling high truly is.

So how is it, if buying low and selling high is so simple to understand yet so difficult to implement that virtually no one can do it consistently, that anyone could honestly expect to master any aspect of trading from this introductory report?

The key is that we're going to <u>CHANGE THE RULES</u>! No longer will you simply buy and sell an asset (an asset would be a stock, a mutual fund or a bond, or even a futures contract) based on what you think is going to happen. Rather, we're going to make an incredible departure from trying to predict the future.

Instead, you'll learn one simple way to put the odds in your favor every time you trade. You'll also learn how to invest just a little to earn a tremendous amount of money if you're right, but lose just a little if you're wrong.

If Making Money Trading Options Was Easy We'd All Be Millionaires

You've probably heard of options. They've been around for decades. You've also probably heard stories of those who trade options. Those stories run from one extreme to the other. That's because the leverage one can get from options is incredible.

In some cases, people have made millions using options. Top notch professional option traders can literally earn millions of dollars in profits each and every year. I personally know of several whose trading operations regularly earn profits in the tens of millions of dollars.

Success is not isolated to the pros. Even novices can hit the big one. Perhaps you know of someone who bought an option and had it quadruple in value in a matter of days

At the other extreme, however, it is a fact that many people have *lost* millions trading options. You see, options are a zero-sum game*. What that means is, for every dollar someone wins, some other trader loses a dollar. So when you hear about someone buying an option for $100 and selling it for $1,100 you can *also* be assured that someone sold the option to that particular buyer for $100. That option seller is also probably looking at a $1,000 loss! If that same trader sold 100 options instead of just one, then his loss would be about $100,000! As this example shows, if you don't control your losses, you could be ruined financially while someone else prospers.

Another common practice on the path to financial ruin is repetitive losing. I just briefly described to you how someone could lose

---

* - There are, of course, exceptions to every rule. When options are used in a strategy that combine options with the underlying asset, it is not a zero-sum game.

big selling options. Unfortunately, just reversing the process — buying options – does *not* guarantee success. You see, buying options that are likely to triple and quadruple in price guarantees that the odds are against you. [More on that later when we learn how options gain and lose value.] In other words, you will "hit a home run" every now and then. But more often, you'll "strike out". The problem is that few investors have the patience or tolerance to sustain a long string of losing trades while waiting for a monster winner. What typically happens is that they give up before hitting it big.

Both of these latter scenarios are, unfortunately, far more common for individuals than those "get rich" stories. The sad fact is that most people lose money, and in some cases, they lose big. But that's because most option traders simply buy a call if they think the market is going up, or buy a put if they think the market is going down.

The dismal performance of individuals trading options should come as no surprise. Very few people know the *name* of the formula that professional traders use to correctly value an option. Even *less* actually know the precise formula itself. Is it any wonder, then, that novices would lose big if they're buying and selling something that they couldn't put a value on?

<u>Putting The Probabilities On Your Side</u>

As we noted earlier, trading options has its ups and downs. For most traders, the wild swings are just too much for most to handle, both mentally and financially. But there are some very attractive aspects inherent in options.

First, the leverage available with options is enormous. The return you can earn on your investment is enormous, whether you are a buyer or a seller.

Also, buyers of options have limited risk. This is one of the most attractive aspects of options.

And sellers of options automatically put the probability of profit in their favor when they implement a position.

Our goal in this book is to show you the "hows" and "whys" of option trading. As you'll learn, once you master the options market, you will be in a position to change the rules of the game so that guessing market direction is no longer a concern.

Think of the following scenario. The stock market has just dropped 10% in the last two weeks. Should you buy more or should you sell everything? If you buy more, the only way to make money is if it goes up. In other words, your investment pays off only if you guessed that market's future *direction* correctly. If you guessed wrong, you lose. The problem is, as noted earlier, most people guess wrong! Thus, when it comes to guessing market direction, most traders are losers.

Let's look at another scenario. Over the past ten years, the market has gone up or down more than 5% in a month only 15 times! In other words, if the S&P 500 was at 600 at the beginning of the month, in order for it to move up or down more than 5% in a month, it would have to be above 630, or below 570. Of the 120 months during the past ten years, such a move out of that range occurred only 15 times! That's only 12.5% of the time. That means the S&P stayed within a 5% range 87.5% of the time!!

Figure 1

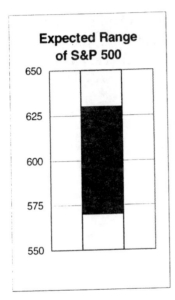

Expected Range of S&P 500

The dark area represents a range of + or -5%, assuming that the S&P 500 is at 600. During the past decade, the month-to-month change in the S&P has been less than five percent 87.5% of the time. The month to month change has exceeded five percent only 12.5% of the time.

That final figure is critical. Because it means, if we can find a strategy that makes money as long as the market stays within that range, we will *automatically* have a strategy that has, historically, made money 87.5% of the time!

By utilizing a strategy of this sort, <u>**we've changed the rules of the game!**</u> No longer are we concerned about the market's trend, its cycle wave, its chart pattern or any other factors. All we're concerned about is its expected range, or the *magnitude* of the market's move.

This is how the rules have changed. We don't care if the market goes up or down. We only care about the size of the market's price fluctuations[1].

To implement a strategy that profits from market magnitude instead of market direction, you need to understand how options work. That's where our next chapter begins.

I think you'll agree with me that the journey will be well worth it. Because once you understand how options work, you will be able to *automatically* improve your probabilities, and put the option trading odds in your favor.

---

[1] It is important to note that we are using the S&P 500 as an example. This methodology can be applied to any market, to any stock or to any stock index. Each market, however, needs to be individually analyzed for prior historical price fluctuations.

<u>What Is An Option?</u>

What is an option? Whether it is in the financial world or any other domain of our existence, quite simply, an option is exactly what its name implies – a choice. Anyone who has an option has a choice. The only thing that differentiates one option from another is defined by the possible choices. For example, the person that arrives at a fork in the road can turn right or left. They have the choice. They have an option.

<u>In the financial world options give you the right to buy or sell at a pre-determined price during a preset time period.</u> As the owner of the option, you have the *choice* of actually buying or selling, <u>or</u> doing nothing. You pay someone for those rights.

In this introductory section, we're going to make extensive use of real estate as an example because of most people's familiarity with it. Later on, we'll get into the "financial asset" aspect of trading options, including options on stocks, options on stock indexes, and options on futures. But first, let's master the basics using something so common, nearly everyone is accustomed to it.

Let's say there is a vacant piece of farm land. The land is worth about $100,000 now. But you think there is going to be a real estate boom in the area during the next few months. You think that the land is going to be worth far more than $100,000. You go to the owner and say, "I want the right to buy this land for $120,000 at anytime during the next year." The owner says, "Okay, but I require $10,000 to grant you the option to buy my property at that price."

The reason the owner requires compensation is because he is giving up the potential for a huge profit while still carrying the bulk of the financial risk during the next 12 months. Here's why that asset owner feels he deserves compensation:

Let's say that there is a real estate bonanza, and a highway interchange gets built. Fast food restaurants and hotels start searching for building sites. They go to the owner of the land. McDonald's steps up and says, we want your land, we'll pay you $500,000. The farm land owner says, "Fine, I'd like to sell it to you. But I'm sorry, I have granted someone an option on the land for the next 12 months. I am obliged to sell it to him for $120,000 during that time. You need to talk to him." McDonald's then contacts the option holder (you) and they tell you that they want to buy the land for $500,000. You can then exercise your right to buy the land for $120,000, paying the farmer the agreed upon price, and then instantly sell the land to McDonald's for $500,000. Your profit in the deal: $380,000. Your cost: $10,000. As you can see, the return potential is astronomical.

Figure 2

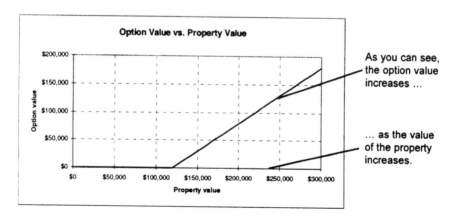

As you can see, the option value increases ...

... as the value of the property increases.

Let's now take a look at what happens if things don't go precisely as planned.

Let's say that the interchange gets built, but while they're digging, they come across a toxic waste dump that nobody knew about. The land is now worthless. The owner now comes to you and says, "I want you to buy the land for $120,000." **But you say,** "I don't care to buy it. And I have the *right*, but *not* the obligation to buy it. I choose not to exercise my right at this time."

As you can see, the land owner, at this point, is stuck with worthless property. Sure, you've lost your $10,000. But the landowner has seen his property value drop by $100,000.

This is a classic example of how options give the option buyer incredible leverage with limited downside risk. As an owner of an option, you can control an asset worth an enormous amount of money for only "pennies on the dollar". By only putting down $10,000, you can control an asset that has *unlimited* profit potential. Because you have so little capital tied up, yet having complete control of the asset, you can earn extraordinary returns on your money. Better still, your risk is limited to the amount of money you put up. As the example illustrates, someone who actually owns the asset has much more risk than the option owner.

You might think, based on the following examples, that option buyers are destined for riches when they're right, and lose only a little when they're wrong. In essence, that is correct. The key, however, is how *often* they are right.

For example, how often is a piece of property you buy suddenly on McDonalds' real estate wish list? And how often do people discover hidden toxic waste dumps on land they wish to buy? Not very often, in either case.

Instead, the most likely scenario is that the land will increase in value, perhaps as much as 10% over the next year. That means, 12 months from now, the land will be worth $110,000. That being the case, you would not want to exercise the option, because you have the right to buy the property for $120,000. Since it is worth only $110,000, you choose not to exercise the option. [Why buy anything for $120,000 when it is only worth $110,000?] In this instance, you, the option buyer, have just lost the $10,000 you gave the option seller for the right to buy the property.

The person who sold you the option, on the other hand, has just pocketed an extra $10,000 for doing nothing more than selling you a right to do something that was unlikely to happen.

This is why, more often than not, option buyers tend to lose money.

Figure 3

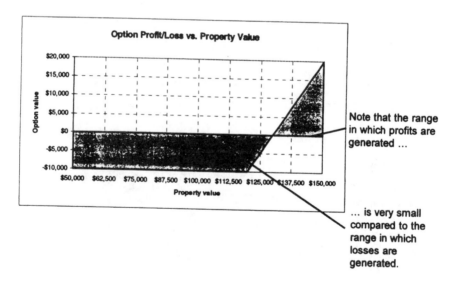

Note that the range in which profits are generated ...

... is very small compared to the range in which losses are generated.

Understanding Option Terminology

The best way to understand option market jargon is to look at and understand each component as we go along. In our real estate example, you can tell that there are certain factors that influence the price we're willing to pay for the right to buy a piece of property. Here are those factors:

1. The duration of the option.

2. The agreed upon price at which the option can be exercised (known as the strike price).

3. The current value of the asset.

4. The cost of money (i.e., interest rates).

5. The risk potential and the reward potential of the asset.

Let's look at each one of these factors individually.

The duration of the option is a factor for logical reasons. If you want to control an asset for five years instead of one year, it would naturally cost more to control it for a longer period of time. Conversely, if you wanted to control the asset for only a day, it would naturally cost less.

The reason for this is due to the fact that the longer you control the asset, the more likely it is that things can happen to influence its price. For example, if you controlled the property for a day, it isn't too likely that a big real estate deal involving your property will be announced that day. Thus it isn't too likely that the price will change while you control the property with your option. If you controlled the property for ten years, however, it is quite possible that during a ten year span some sort of real estate deal could develop. Therefore it is possible for the property to have a significant price change during the period you control it with your option. For that reason, as the duration of the option increases, the value of the option also increases.

The price at which an option can be exercised is a factor for the following reason. Let's say that you want to acquire an option to buy a piece of property. You can agree to buy the property at $100,000, or you can agree to buy the property at $200,000. If both options cost the same, which one would be more attractive? The option with the $100,000 exercise[2] price. The reason is simple.

Let's assume that the property increased in value to $150,000. If you had the right to buy the property for $100,000, you could "exercise" your right, purchase the property for $100,000, and then sell it for $150,000, thus earning a profit of $50,000. If, however, you had the right to buy the property for $200,000 and you "exercised" your right, you'd purchase the property for $200,000, sell it for $150,000, creating a <u>loss</u> of $50,000. Needless to say, you would not "exercise" your right to buy if you owned the option with a $200,000 exercise price. You'd do nothing because there would be no profit in it.

The fact that there would be a $50,000 profit on the option with a $100,000 "exercise" price and no profit on the option with a $200,000 "exercise" price illustrates how an option's value should increase or decrease, depending upon the agreed upon price at

---

[2] An option's exercise price (also known as its strike price) is the price agreed upon by both the option buyer and the seller at which the option buyer can exercise his or her right to buy the asset (or sell, in the case of a put option [more on that later]).

which the option can be exercised.

The current value of the asset is an obvious factor, and here's why. Let's say that you wanted an option to buy a piece of property for $100,000 (*Hint: Remember, the $100,000 figure is also known as the exercise price, or strike price*) sometime during the next year. The property you're looking at is worth $20,000. During the year you own the option, property values <u>double</u>. The property is now worth $40,000. As the owner of the option, you still would not make money, even though real estate prices double. That's because you would never exercise your right to buy the property for $100,000 when it is worth only $40,000.

On the other hand, if the property was worth $80,000 to start, and property values doubled, the property would now be worth $160,000. As the owner of the option, you have the right to buy the property for $100,000. Therefore, you could exercise your right, buy the property for $100,000, and then sell it for $160,000, earning $60,000[3].

What this illustrates is how the current price of the asset impacts the value of the option. In both instances, the price of the asset doubled in value. But because one asset's price was higher, and, therefore, closer to the exercise price, the option had value ($60,000 at expiration). In the other instance, where the price was lower, and, therefore, further away from the exercise price, when the asset price doubled, the option had no value. Consequently, in the case of options that give you the right to buy an asset, the higher the asset's price, the more valuable the option.

---

[3] Note: The $60,000 figure, the amount you would earn if you exercised your option, is called the "INTRINSIC VALUE" of an option.

Thus far, the factors we have covered are not all that startling, even to relative newcomers. The fact that time and price influence an option's value should come as no surprise. The other two factors, however, are somewhat esoteric.

The cost of money, while esoteric, is not difficult to understand. By the way, the cost of money is nothing more than the prevailing interest rate. Here's what we mean. Let's say you are contemplating buying an option on a piece of land. You are considering giving someone $10,000 for a right to buy the property over the next year. If you hold the option for a year, your $10,000 is tied up with the option seller for the entire year. That means, if your money is tied up somewhere besides an interest-bearing bank account, you are not collecting the interest on the $10,000 that you could, if you didn't buy the option. Thus, buying an option costs you lost income. If the prevailing interest rate on a one-year Treasury bill was 5%, then you'd be passing up a guaranteed $500 by buying the option. As you can see, the current rate of interest is important when valuing an option, because it represents what's known as "opportunity cost". That is, the opportunity cost of money represents how much of a guaranteed return you are passing up by investing in an option instead of a T-bill. As interest rates vary, so does that opportunity cost.

Also, from a different point of view, options allow you to control an asset without actually paying for the asset. What that means is that you don't tie up a lot of money to buy the asset itself. Instead, you can use that money to invest in an interest bearing account and earn income on those proceeds. Thus, by buying an option, you eliminate the "opportunity cost" of owning the asset.

The final factor is the reward and risk potential of the underlying asset. In our example, we were buying an option on a piece of real estate. That piece of property in our example is called the underlying asset.

In this next example, we're going to look at two different pieces of property. Property One is in the middle of a major metropolitan area; prices have already climbed substantially and the whole area is still experiencing rapid growth. Its current value is $100,000. Property Two is in the middle of the forest; there are no cities anywhere near, no roads for mining or timber equipment, and no development opportunities in the immediate future. Its current value is also $100,000.

If you could lock in a price, controlling either property and profiting from further price appreciation, while limiting your risk to an identical amount in the event real estate suddenly fell on hard times, on which property would you like to have an option?

Well, ask yourself this, "Which one is *likely* to climb from $100,000 to $200,000 in the next few years?" The answer to that question is obvious – the metropolitan property is more likely to double in value. That *likelihood* of gaining in value directly impacts an option's price.

Remember, if you buy an option, you are acquiring the right to buy an underlying asset (in this case, property) at a preset, agreed upon price during a preset, agreed upon time span. Therefore, if both properties are currently priced at $100,000, and the options on both properties are five years in duration, and in both cases, the exercise price at which the property can be purchased is $130,000, then the amount of money you would be willing to pay to control the metropolitan property should be higher than the amount you would be willing to pay in order to control the forest land.

That's because the reward potential on the metropolitan property is higher than the reward potential of the forest land. Also, the probability of reward is higher on the metropolitan property than it is on the forest property.

You see, it is reasonably certain that a good piece of commercial property will increase in value by 30% during the next five years. Therefore it is highly probable that you will be able to exercise your option for some value during the next five years, as it is highly probable that the property would be worth more than $130,000 (the price at which you have the right to buy the property, no matter how high its actual market price) during the next five years.

It is much less certain that a piece of forest land with no access roads, and with little development potential, would increase in value by 30% over the next five years. [Certainly it's possible, but not nearly as probable as the commercial property.] Therefore, it is less probable that you would want to exercise your option on the forest property than on the commercial property.

Because it is more likely that the option on the forest property will be worthless in five years, one would not want to pay as much for that option as they would for the option on the commercial property, which is almost certain to have value in five years.

Therefore, it can be stated that, all other factors being equal, options on assets with high reward potential will tend to have more value than options on assets with low reward potential. That is, the higher the reward potential (and, likewise, the higher the risk potential) of the underlying asset, the higher the price of the option.

This example illustrates how the reward potential of an underlying asset directly impacts the value of an option. Which is just one of five factors that impact the value of an option.

In review, the five factors that impact an option's value are:

1. The duration of the option.

2. The agreed upon price at which the option can be exercised.

3. The current value of the asset.

4. The cost of money (i.e., interest rates).

5. The risk potential and the reward potential of the asset (in the world of options on stocks and futures, this is known as volatility)

These "value factors" hold true for any option on any underlying asset, whether it is real estate, stocks or commodities. This leads us into our next topic, and that is options on "listed[4]" assets. So far, we've talked about options on real estate. While options on real estate are quite common, they are hard for the average person to "trade" because real estate is relatively "illiquid".

---

[4] Listed simply means that an asset is available for trading on an exchange.

Trading Options on Exchange Listed Assets

What we mean by "illiquid" is that it is often a time-intensive process for a seller of real estate to find a buyer. The same thing goes for buyers trying to find sellers of property they want to purchase. Often, you have to search far and wide, using an agent, and then you have to spend time with attorneys and bankers, not to mention the negotiating process with the seller to finally come up with a transaction price.

There just isn't any centralized marketplace where you can simply pick up the phone and say "sell" and have your house instantly sold.

When it comes to stocks and commodities, however, there *are* centralized locations to buy and sell instantly. Those locations are called exchanges. Most people have heard of Wall Street. That's the location of the New York Stock Exchange and the American Stock Exchange.

Chicago is the location of the biggest exchanges for commodity traders — The Chicago Board of Trade and the Chicago Mercantile Exchange. Back in the early-1970s, traders at the Chicago Board of Trade got together and decided to begin trading options on stocks. This eventually led to the world's busiest options exchange, The Chicago Board Options Exchange.

Currently, there are four U.S. exchanges that trade options on stocks, stock indexes, interest rate products and currencies. Those exchanges are: The Chicago Board Options Exchange, The American Stock Exchange, The Philadelphia Stock Exchange, and The Pacific Stock Exchange.

One reason that exchanges can provide you with instantaneous purchase and sale transactions is because the products available for purchase and sale are identical. That is, one share of IBM is identical to another share of IBM.

Obviously, this could never be true of real estate. That's because each property is different, with its own set of individual advantages and disadvantages. Because no property is identical, you simply can't buy and sell, sight unseen.

But with exchange-traded products, you can buy and sell sight unseen, because you know that every share of Ford is going to be exactly like every other share of Ford. So when you want to sell, someone else can buy with confidence.

A market that offers the ability to instantly enter and exit positions at a reasonable price is said to have "liquidity".

The other advantage to exchanges is that they eliminate counter-party risk. Take for example the real estate transaction. Typically, you've got to set up a meeting, with an attorney present, sign dozens of contracts and forms, and make payments only with bank-certified checks. Then and only then does the property change ownership. The reason for all of this is to prevent, as much as possible, one party to the transaction from defrauding the other party to the transaction.

The bank certified check is a classic example of this. It protects the seller by reducing the chance that the buyer might present a bogus check.

Needless to say, when you pick up the phone to buy or sell a stock, you aren't being asked to present a certified check. That's because the brokerage firm instantly acts upon your request, and the exchange guarantees the trade.

Let's say a trader places an order to buy an option. What happens is that the order goes to the exchange, and then someone sells that trader the option. If the buyer then backs out of the trade, the seller has *still* sold the option. That's because the exchange and the broker guarantee that the trade has been executed and both will stand behind it. Essentially, the trader has bought the option. But if the option buyer suddenly backs out of the trade, the brokerage firm has become the buyer of the option. If for some unforeseen reason the brokerage firm can't meet the obligation, then the exchange itself and its many members stand behind the trade.

This multiple level of redundancy on "listed" stocks, futures and options is one of the key ingredients to having a successful marketplace. Many traders take it for granted, but it is the one critical factor that gives traders around the globe enough confidence, so that when they pick up the telephone to place an order, they know that they are getting exactly what they ordered. And they *don't* have to worry about the performance of the person taking the other side of their trade.

A recent example occurred in 1987. The stock market crashed in October of that year and many option traders got wiped out. It was so bad that these traders were unable to meet their commitments. That left the brokerage firms to make up the difference. Some smaller firms were unable to handle the financial stress, which meant that the exchange members had to meet the commitment individual traders were unable to meet. The next day, the Federal Reserve Board stepped in and strongly hinted, in a very carefully worded, prepared statement, that banks go ahead and loan as much money as needed to exchange member firms, so that the exchange members could meet the financial obligations of all traders. With those words, counterparty risk was eliminated and a crisis was averted.

Selling High, *Then* Buying Low
How to reverse the typical transaction process
and make money from falling prices

Some of you may have heard of this before, some of you may not have heard of it. In the world of finance, there is a transaction you can implement known as "selling short". It is a way of profiting from falling prices. Here's how it works:

Let's say that you were looking at a company – some high flier called ABC Tech. You felt ABC stock had gone up too far, too fast. You also noticed in the company's annual report that there were some shenanigans going on that were unnoticed by others. You felt that the company's shares, now priced at $80, were likely to fall sharply. You wanted to make money as the price of the stock fell.

What you do is "sell short". To do that you first borrow the shares, usually from your broker. You then sell the shares you borrowed in the open market, in this case at $80. Remember, whenever you sell something, you collect money. In this case, you collect $80.

At this point, we need to ask a simple question in order to understand how we make money. That question is, what is our risk?

The answer is, if we've borrowed the shares, the person who loaned the shares to us may ask for them back. And that's how we make or lose money.

Think of it this way: if the price of ABC Tech drops to $50 and the brokerage firm that loaned us the stock asks for it to be returned, we've got to give it back to them. Since we already sold it at $80, then to return the stock, we've got to buy it in the open market. We buy it back for $50. But remember, we've already collected $80. So our net profit is $30!

Let's go through this one more time. It may help to visualize a checking account to better understand this.

1. First, you borrow the shares. This shows up as neither a debit or a credit.

2. Next, you sell the shares in the open market and collect the money. Whenever you sell anything, you receive money. Money given to you shows up as a credit on your checking account statement and your brokerage statement.

3. Later, you buy back the shares that you borrowed. Whenever you buy anything, money comes out of your pocket. This shows up as a debit to your account.

4. Finally, you return the shares to the person from whom you borrowed the stock.

Here's how the arithmetic of a typical short sale transaction looks, using a round-lot of 100 shares:

Transaction	Result
Borrow 100 shares of ABC Tech (price 80)	0.00
Sell 100 shares of ABC Tech at 80	+8,000.00
Buy 100 shares of ABC Tech at 50	-5,000.00
Return the 100 shares of ABC Tech you borrowed	0.00
Net Profit or Loss	**+3,000.00**

That's what it looks like if things go right and the stock drops. But what if the stock price rises. Let's say you borrowed the stock, sold it at $80, thus collecting $80, which shows up as a credit to your account. At some point, the person who loaned you the stock will call and say, "I want my stock back." You then have to buy the shares in the open market, and return the stock to the person who loaned you the stock. If the ABC Tech went up to $100, you will have to pay $100. The purchase shows up as a debit. So your account has a credit of $80 and a debit of $100. The net result is that you have a total net debit of $20, which means $20 has been debited from your account. In other words, the stock went up and you lost. Here's how the arithmetic looks, using a round-lot of 100 shares:

Transaction	Result
Borrow 100 shares of ABC Tech (price 80)	0.00
Sell 100 shares of ABC Tech at 80	+8,000.00
Buy 100 shares of ABC Tech at 100	-10,000.00
Return the 100 shares of ABC Tech you borrowed	0.00
Net Profit or Loss	**-2,000.00**

Let's look at a couple of more examples. Let's say you are looking at a toy company. You hear that the Christmas selling season is going to be a disaster. You also hear that video games are stealing thunder from traditional toy makers. Plus, this particular toy company, XYZ Toys, makes toys your kids don't like. You think that the stock is going to go down. XYZ Toys is currently trading at 25. You sell short 200 shares.

A few weeks later, the market proves you right. XYZ Toys is now trading at 15. You take profits of $2,000.

Here's the arithmetic:

Transaction	Result
Borrow 200 shares of XYZ Toys (price 25)	0.00
Sell 200 shares of XYZ Toys at 25	+5,000.00
Buy 200 shares of XYZ Toys at 15	-3,000.00
Return the 200 shares of XYZ Toys you borrowed	0.00
Net Profit or Loss	**+2,000.00**

Let's say you suspect that inflation will be benign for the next several months. You think that gold, being an inflation hedge, will decline in price. You also think that the weakness in gold will spill over into gold stocks. Right now Barrick Gold, one of the biggest gold producers, is trading at $30. You decide to sell short 500 shares.

A few weeks later, the latest inflation data is released. It shows that inflation is virtually non-existent, and the price of gold drops, taking most gold stocks with it. Barrick Gold is now trading at $20. You decide to exit your "short" position, at a tidy profit of $5,000.

Here's the arithmetic:

Transaction	Result
Borrow 500 shares of ABX (price 30)	0.00
Sell 500 shares of ABX at 30	+15,000.00
Buy 500 shares of ABX at 20	-10,000.00
Return the 500 shares of ABX you borrowed	0.00
Net Profit or Loss	**+5,000.00**

One final example — this one will show us why short selling is so dangerous.

Let's say there is an airline, L-M Air. L-M Air is experiencing some problems. There are safety concerns, their planes are old, they're deep in debt, all of which is causing a public relations nightmare and near-empty planes. You think that the company is headed for bankruptcy, so you sell 500 shares short. L-M Air shares are trading for $10.

One evening, a few weeks later, Goliath Air announces that they want to buy the company. Goliath needs the gate space desperately. Goliath has agreed to sell the older airplanes to an air-freight shipper once the purchase of L-M Air is finalized. Goliath doesn't want any other airline to get in the way, and they don't want L-M's Board of Directors to reject the bid, so they offer an extremely high price: $30.

The next day, before the market opens for trading, Leviathan Air announces that they don't want to see their arch-rival, Goliath, succeed in acquiring those gates. The market suspects that Leviathan will make a competing offer for L-M Air. Later that morning, L-M Air shares open for trading at $35. Your brokerage firm, the one from whom you borrowed the shares, calls you to tell you that they want the shares back (or more money). Can you figure out what just happened to your investment?

Here's the arithmetic:

Transaction	Result
Borrow 500 shares of LM (price 10)	0.00
Sell 500 shares of LM at 10	+5,000.00
Buy 500 shares of LM at 35	-17,500.00
Return the 500 shares of LM you borrowed	0.00
Net Profit or Loss	**-12,500.00**

You just lost $12,500 on an investment that had a *maximum* profit potential of $5,000. The fact that you can lose substantially more than you can gain, that your loss potential is unlimited, is why short selling is best left to experienced traders.

One thing to note about short selling — the borrowing and returning of shares is "transparent". That is, <u>the person selling short doesn't ever see the borrowing and selling aspects of the transaction on their statement</u> (although they will see the *impact* of it when they look at the margin interest section of their statement). All the short seller sees is that they sell something at the inception of the trade, and that they buy it back at a later date to close out the trade.

Review

Before we go any further, let's take a quick opportunity to review what we've covered so far:

1. Options give you the right to buy or sell an asset at a predetermined price during a specified time period.

2. There are five factors that impact an option's value.

3. Selling short is a method by which you can make money from falling prices.

4. By using a particular type of option strategy, you can construct a trade that *automatically* puts the probabilities in your favor.

5. Exchange-traded options give you the benefit of instant liquidity and eliminate counter-party risk.

The next several chapters are designed to give you a thorough understanding of how the option trading process works and how profits and losses from trading are generated. The process involves a comprehensive review of valuing calls and puts, and then calculating the profits and losses from buying and selling options.

THE CALCULATIONS ARE EXTREMELY EASY. But they can also be rather tedious. During the monotony, please don't lose sight of our ultimate goal – to make money from trading – something very few traders <u>ever</u> achieve.

The following chapters are an essential first step on the path towards consistent profits. If the process ever seems tiresome, just remember why you got this book, and think about how trading options profitably and consistently could change your life forever.

Offsetting Transactions

It is extremely important to note that what we're going to do is calculate the exercise value of the options. You do *not* need to exercise your option in order to realize a profit (e.g., turn a profit on paper into an actual profit in real dollars and cents).

As noted earlier, options are traded on major stock and commodity exchanges world wide. Traders buy and sell options all the time. Almost always, options trade at or above their exercise value (there are some rare exceptions).

Because of this, if you had an option that had an exercise value of, say, $400, you could pretty much guarantee that instead of exercising the option, you could sell it on one of the options exchanges for at least $400.

When you sell an option that you've already bought, it is called an offsetting transaction.

You can also short sell options. That is, you can sell them at the inception of the trade and buy them back later. If you sell an option short, the transaction to close out the position is a "buy" or a "purchase". That purchase is also called an offsetting transaction.

Because of the availability of offsetting transactions, few options are ever exercised. Almost all options are offset. Options that are bought are usually sold, and options that are sold short are usually repurchased. The ability to offset an "opening" transaction via a "closing" transaction is an important feature that makes it simple to trade options without worrying about the headache of actually exercising the option.

Types of Options and Determining Their Values - Part I - Calls

As everyone knows, there are two types of transactions – buying and selling.

There are also two types of options. So far we've covered the type that gives the buyer of the option the right to buy the asset. That type of an option is known as a **call option**.

It is called a "call option" because the owner of the option can do just that, call away the underlying asset. That is, the option owner can call upon the seller of the option to deliver the asset, provided the option buyer pays the agreed upon exercise price. The seller (also called the *grantor*) of a call option has the *obligation* to sell the asset to you at the preset price.

Let's look at an example of a call option, this time using a stock, instead of real estate, as our asset.

It is October. You think that the market will rally into the end of the year. General Electric shares tend to rise and fall with the market, so you think that GE will go up with the market. Let's assume GE is currently trading at 100. You want to acquire the right to buy GE shares if they increase in value between now and the Christmas holidays, so you buy a call option with a strike price of 100 and an expiration date of December 20. Remember, the strike price is the price at which the option can be exercised. This means that you will have the right to buy GE shares at 100 before the December options expire on December 20, no matter how high or how low GE shares are.

The seller of the option, who will be obliged to deliver to you the shares of GE if you ask for them, requires compensation for giving you the right to buy GE at 100. The compensation you give him (e.g., the price of the option you pay) is called the **option premium**. The price of the option in October is 5. That's $1/20^{th}$ of the price of the stock itself. So your out-of-pocket expenses are substantially reduced when compared to buying the stock.

Now let's fast forward to December. Let's look at what the option will be worth as GE shares fluctuate. Remember, the December call option with a strike price of 100 gives you the right but not the obligation to buy GE shares at 100 before December 20.

If GE shares are trading at 80 on the New York Stock Exchange, would you want to exercise your right, call away the stock and pay 100? Of course not. Why would you want to pay 100 when the market price of GE is 80? Therefore, when GE shares are at 80, the option has no "exercise" value. In this case, it would be worthless at expiration.

How about if GE is trading at 90? Same thing. No one would want to pay 100, as is your right, if you can buy GE in the open market at 90. Therefore, when GE shares are at 90, the option has no "exercise" value. In this case, it would be worthless at expiration.

In both instances, there is no value in exercising the option. This brings up a term that you will hear more about, "out-of-the-money". **Out-of-the-money** options are options that have no value if the option were to be exercised.

What if GE shares were at 100? In this case, it really doesn't matter. You could either buy the shares in the open market for 100, or exercise your option for 100. At the very least, one could state that there is no *added* value to exercising the option, so it is essentially worthless. An option whose exercise price is identical to the current market price is said to be "**at-the-money**".

How about 110? You could exercise your right to "call" away GE and buy it at the agreed upon exercise price of 100 and then instantly sell the shares in the open market at 110. In this case, you make 10 from exercising your option. Options that can be exercised for any value are called **in-the-money** options.

Finally, what happens if GE shares go to 120? Again, you could exercise your right to "call" away and buy the shares at 100, sell them at 120, making 20 from the exercise.

This "exercise value" goes by another term used by option traders. It is called "intrinsic value".

Here is a plot of the option's intrinsic value:

Figure 4

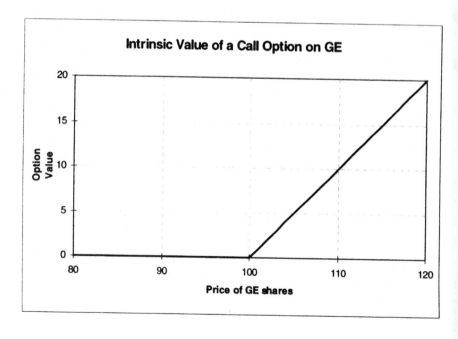

Notice that the call option's value is zero until the price of GE climbs above 100.

In this book, we are not going to get into commodity options in depth. But I do want to say that they work in the very same way as stock options work. The only difference is that commodity options are options on futures contracts, not options on stocks. Therefore, if you exercise a commodity option that is not cash-settled, you will be delivered a futures contract, not shares of stock.

Types of Options and Determining Their Values - Part II - Puts

Let's review what we've covered so far. There are two types of transactions – buying and selling. Also, we know that there is at least one type of option — a call option. A call option gives the holder of the option the right to buy. As we showed, call options tend to increase in value as the price of the underlying asset increases in value.

As you might surmise, since there is an option that gives you the right to do one type of transaction (in the case of a call option, it gives you the right to buy), there is also an option that gives you the right to do the other type of transaction. That option is called a put option.

A **put option** gives the holder of the option the right, but not the obligation, to sell the underlying asset at specific price during a preset period of time.

When you have the right to sell, the other party to the transaction has the *obligation* to buy. That is why it is called a put – because you are "putting" the asset into the hands of the option seller at the agreed upon exercise price. This causes <u>put options to increase in value as the price of the asset drops</u>.

Let's take a look at our earlier example of GE to see how puts work and why they gain value when the underlying asset price drops.

It is September. You know that the stock market has shown an extremely powerful seasonal tendency to drop during September and October. Because GE shares tend to rise and fall with the market, you want to own an option that *rises in value when the market falls*. You want to own a put option.

GE is trading at 100 in September. You want to acquire the right to sell GE shares if they drop in value, so you buy a put option with a strike price of 100 and an expiration date of October 18 (stock options and stock index options expire on the third Friday of every month). Remember, the strike price is the price at which the option can be exercised. This means that you will have the right to sell GE shares at 100 before the October options expire on October 18, no matter how high or how low GE shares are.

The seller of the option, who will be obliged to buy from you the shares of GE if you want to sell, requires compensation for giving you the right to sell GE to him at 100. The compensation you give him (e.g. the price of the option you pay) is called the option premium. The price of the option in September is 3.

Now let's fast forward to October. Let's look at what the option will be worth as GE shares fluctuate. Remember, the October put option with a strike price of 100 gives you the right but not the obligation to sell GE shares at 100 before October 18.

If GE shares are trading at 80 on the New York Stock Exchange, here's what would happen. You would have the right to sell the stock to the person who sold you the option. The price at which you would sell GE would be the exercise price of 100. Remember, the person who sells the option has the obligation to buy it from you at the preset price. Therefore, you could buy the stock in the open market at 80 and immediately sell it to the option grantor at 100, as is your right under the option. By buying GE at 80 and immediately selling it for 100, your net is 20. Therefore, the exercise value of a put option with strike price of 100 is 20 when the asset is at 80.

What about when GE is at 90? You could buy the stock at 90 in the open market, and exercise your right to sell the stock to the option grantor at 100. When you buy at 90 and sell at 100, you earn 10, which is the option's value.

How about if GE is trading at 100? In this case, it really doesn't matter. You could buy the shares in the open market for 100, and exercise your right to sell them at 100. But that would merely be a breakeven transaction. At the very least, one could state that there is no added value to exercising the option, so it is essentially worthless. As with a call option, any option whose exercise price is identical to the current market price is said to be "**at-the-money**".

How about if GE was at 110? You could exercise your right to put the stock to the option seller. But why would you? If you bought GE at 110, your right would be to sell it at 100. And why would anybody buy anything at 110, only to sell it at 100? It automatically locks in a loss of -10. Because you have the right and are not obliged to do this, you would do nothing – the option is worthless.

Finally, what happens if GE shares go to 120? Your right is to sell GE at 100. But GE shares are trading at 120. So you would have to pay 120, only to sell the shares at 100, thus locking in a loss of -20. Because you have the right and are not obliged to do this, the option is worthless.

Here is a plot of the put's intrinsic value:

Figure 5

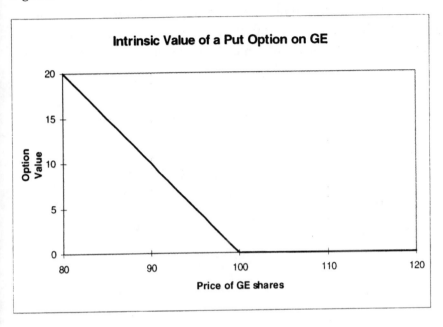

As you can see through this example, a put's exercise value increases as the price of the underlying asset decreases. It does so by giving the option holder the right to sell at a predetermined price. When the price of the asset drops, the option holder can buy the asset at the current market price, put the asset into the option grantor's hands (i.e., sell it to the option grantor), and collect the agreed-upon sale price, which is the strike price of the option.

Calculating Profits and Losses on Option Trades

Up to now, we've discovered what an option is, what types of options there are, and how options gain or lose value. The next step is to determine how an option transaction impacts your bottom line.

A quick example would be, if you bought something for 3 and sold it (via an offsetting transaction) for 6, you'd have a profit of 3. This is calculated in the following manner: You spent 3 to buy something. Whenever you buy something, you pay someone, taking money out of your account, so it shows up as a debit. Once you've purchased something, you need to sell it via an offsetting transaction to turn a paper profit into a real profit. When you sell this particular item, you sell it for 6. Whenever you sell something, you get money. Money goes into your account, so it shows up as a credit. Therefore the 3 appears as a (-3) minus 3, and the 6 appears as a (+6) plus 6. Add the two together and you get the net profit (or loss). The net profit in this case is +3 (calculated by adding -3 and +6).

Simple enough, but vitally important.

In the next four chapters, we will be providing you with examples that show how to calculate profits and losses on buying and selling puts and calls. Each chapter provides you with two examples. The thought here is that, for the novice, "practice makes perfect".

Because the examples are somewhat redundant, if at any time you feel that you understand the analysis process, feel free to skip ahead to the next chapter.

Calculating Profit and Loss Potential on a Call Option Purchase

Let's quickly review. A call option gives the option buyer the right to buy an underlying asset at a predetermined price. Also, whenever we buy something, we have to give the seller money, so money is debited from our account. When we sell, we receive money from a buyer, so money is credited to our account. After buying something, we need to sell it in order to realize a profit or loss.

Now let's look at a call option purchase. Let's take our original example: the GE call option. It is October, let's assume GE is currently trading at 100. You want to acquire the right to buy GE shares if they increase in value between now and the Christmas holidays, so you buy a call option with a strike price of 100 and an expiration date of December 20. Remember, the strike price is the price at which the option can be exercised. This means that you will have the right to buy GE shares at 100 before the December options expire on December 20, no matter how high or how low GE shares are.

The seller of the option, who will be obliged to deliver to you the shares of GE if you ask for them, requires compensation for giving you the right to buy GE at 100. The compensation you give him (e.g. the price of the option you pay) is called the option premium. **The price of the option in October is 5**. All stock options are worth $100 per point. Therefore the GE option costs $500. If you buy this option, it will show up on your account statement as a debit of $500 (plus commissions).

Now let's fast forward to December. Let's look at what your profit or loss will be as GE shares fluctuate. Remember, the December call option with a strike price of 100 gives you the right but not the obligation to buy GE shares at 100 before December 20.

If GE shares are trading at 80 on the New York Stock Exchange, would you want to exercise your right, call away the stock and pay 100? Of course not. Why would you want to pay 100 when the open market price of GE is 80? Therefore, when GE shares are at 80, the option has no "exercise" value. In this case, it would be worthless at expiration. If you tried to sell the option, no one would want to buy it. So you just let it expire.

If you let the options expire worthless, the transaction looks like this:

Transaction	Result
Buy one GE December 100 call (price 5)	-500.00
GE December 100 call expires worthless	0.00
Net Profit or Loss	**-500.00**

How about if GE is trading at 90? Same thing. No one would want to pay 100, as is your right, if you can buy GE in the open market at 90. Therefore, when GE shares are at 90, the option has no "exercise" value. In this case, it would be worthless at expiration. If you tried to sell the option, no one would want to buy it. You just let it expire.

If you let the options expire worthless, the transaction look like this:

Transaction	Result
Buy one GE December 100 call (price 5)	-500.00
GE December 100 call expires worthless	0.00
Net Profit or Loss	**-500.00**

In both instances, there is no value in exercising the option, so the options expired worthless.

What if GE shares were at 100? In this case, it really doesn't matter. You could either buy the shares in the open market for 100, or exercise your option for 100. At the very least, one could state that there is no added value to exercising the option, so it is essentially worthless. If you tried to sell the option, no one would want to buy it. You just let it expire.

If you let the options expire worthless, the transaction looks like this:

Transaction	Result
Buy one GE December 100 call (price 5)	-500.00
GE December 100 call expires worthless	0.00
Net Profit or Loss	**-500.00**

How about 110? At 110, the options have value. You could exercise your right to "call" away and buy GE at 100 and then instantly sell the shares in the open market at 110. In this case, you make 10 from exercising your option. Also, as we showed, you could simply offset the transaction by selling the option. If you sold the option for its exercise value (10), it would show up on your account as a plus.

If you exercise your option, the transaction would look like this:

Transaction	Result
Buy one GE December 100 call (price 5)	-500.00
Exercise the option (buy 100 shares of GE at 100)	-10,000.00
Sell 100 shares of GE at 110	+11,000.00
Net Profit or Loss	**+500.00**

If you sell the option, the transaction looks like this:

Transaction	Result
Buy one GE December 100 call (price 5)	-500.00
Sell GE December 100 call (price 10)	+1,000.00
Net Profit or Loss	**+500.00**

Finally, what happens if GE shares go to 120? Again, you could exercise your right to "call" away and buy the shares at 100, and then sell them at 120, making 20 from the exercise. Or you could simply sell your option in an offsetting transaction.

If you exercise your option, the transaction would look like this:

Transaction	Result
Buy one GE December 100 call (price 5)	-500.00
Exercise the option (buy 100 shares of GE at 100)	-10,000.00
Sell 100 shares of GE at 120	+12,000.00
Net Profit or Loss	**+1,500.00**

If you sell the option, the transaction looks like this:

Transaction	Result
Buy one GE December 100 call (price 5)	-500.00
Sell GE December 100 call (price 20)	+2,000.00
Net Profit or Loss	**+1,500.00**

Here is a plot of the option purchase's profit and loss as the price of GE fluctuates:

Figure 6

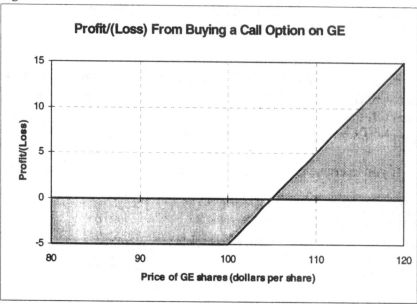

Profit/(Loss) From Buying a Call Option on GE

Remember, the option starts gaining value once GE shares start climbing above 100. But notice how the line does not cross the zero mark until the price of GE reaches 105. This is the option purchase's breakeven. In other words, if GE finishes below 105, the option buyer loses. That's because the option does not gain enough value to overcome the purchase price. If it finishes above 105, the option buyer will earn a profit.

Notice that the breakeven price is equal to the price of the option when purchased (5), plus the option's strike price (100) [5 + 100 = 105]. This is a very simple rule of thumb for calculating the breakeven of a call purchase. The breakeven of a call purchase is equal to the price of the option plus the option's strike price.

Here are the important characteristics of call buying:

1. Small cash outlay - Compared to buying the asset, the cost of a call option is much, much smaller.

2. Bullish bias - The underlying asset *must* go up in order for you to make money.

3. Limited risk - If you're wrong and the underlying asset declines in value, your maximum loss potential is limited to the purchase price of the option.

4. Unlimited profit potential - If you're right about direction, the profit potential is virtually unlimited. The percentage profit available is much larger than the risk potential.

5. Poor probability - As indicated at the beginning of the report, most traders find it almost impossible to accurately guess direction consistently. When you purchase an option, you not only have to be right about market direction, your forecast must take place during a limited amount of time (prior to option expiration). In other words, you *must* guess direction accurately and your forecast *has* to take place quickly.

Calculating Profit and Loss Potential on a Put Option Purchase

Let's quickly review the put option process. A put option gives the put holder the right to sell an underlying asset at a predetermined price in a preset period of time. Because of this, when an underlying asset drops in price, the put holder can buy the asset in the open market at the current price (which is now lower), and, by exercising the put, immediately sell it at a higher price (the predetermined exercise price from when the option was purchased). This gives the put owner the ability to buy low and sell high, thus giving them the ability to earn a profit.

Also, whenever we buy something, we have to give the seller money, so money is debited from our account. When we sell, we receive money from a buyer, so money is credited to our account. After buying something, we need to sell it in order to realize a profit or loss.

Let's take a look at our earlier example of GE to see how we can determine our profit and loss potential from a put purchase.

Recall from our example which showed how to determine the value of a put option, it's September. You know that the stock market has shown an extremely powerful seasonal tendency to drop during September and October. Because GE shares tend to rise and fall with the market, you want to own an option that *rises in value when the market falls*. You want to buy a put option.

GE is trading at 100 in September. You want to acquire the right to sell GE shares if they drop in value, so you buy a put option with a strike price of 100 and an expiration date of October 18 (stock options and stock index options expire on the third Friday of every month). Remember, the strike price is the price at which the option can be exercised. This means that you will have the right to sell GE shares at 100 before the October options expire on October 18, no matter how high or how low GE shares are.

The seller of the option, who will be obliged to buy from you the shares of GE if you want to sell them, requires compensation for giving you the right to sell GE to him at 100. The compensation you give him (e.g. the price of the option you pay) is called the option premium. **The price of the option in September is 3.** All stock options are worth $100 per point. Therefore the GE option costs $300. If you buy this option, it will show up on your account statement as a debit of $300 (plus commissions).

Now let's fast forward to October. Let's look at what our profit/ loss will be as GE shares fluctuate. Remember, the October put option with a strike price of 100 gives you the right but not the obligation to sell GE shares at 100 before October 18.

If GE shares are trading at 80 on the New York Stock Exchange, here's what would happen. As the option buyer, you would have the right to sell the stock to the person who sold you the option at a price of 100. Remember, the person who sells the option has the obligation to buy it from you at the preset price. Therefore, you could buy the stock in the open market at 80 and immediately sell it to the option grantor at 100, as is your right under the option. By buying GE at 80 and immediately selling it for 100, your net is 20. Therefore, the exercise value of a put option with strike price of 100 is 20 when the asset is at 80. So if you exercised your option, you would earn 20 from the exercise. Also, as we showed earlier, you could simply offset the transaction by selling the option. If you sold the option for its exercise value (20), it would show up on your account as a plus.

If you exercise your option, the transaction would look like this (Remember, you bought the option for 3. Stock options are worth

$100 per point):

Transaction	Result
Buy one GE October 100 put (price 3)	-300.00
Buy 100 shares of GE at 80	-8,000.00
Exercise the put (Sell 100 shares of GE at 100)	+10,000.00
Net Profit or Loss	**+1,700.00**

If you sell the option for 20, the transaction looks like this:

Transaction	Result
Buy one GE October 100 put (price 3)	-300.00
Sell GE October 100 put (price 20)	+2,000.00
Net Profit or Loss	**+1,700.00**

What about when GE is at 90? You could buy the stock at 90 in the open market, and exercise your right to sell the stock to the option grantor at 100. When you buy at 90 and sell at 100, you earn 10, which is the option's value. Also, as we showed earlier, you could simply offset the transaction by selling the option. If you sold the option for its exercise value (10), it would show up on your account as a plus.

If you sell the option for 10, the transaction looks like this:

Transaction	Result
Buy one GE October 100 put (price 3)	-300.00
Sell GE October 100 put (price 10)	+1,000.00
Net Profit or Loss	**+700.00**

How about if GE is trading at 100? In this case, it really doesn't matter. You could buy the shares in the open market for 100, and exercise your right to sell them at 100. But that would merely be a breakeven transaction. At the very least, one could state that there is no added value to exercising the option, so it is essentially worthless. In this case, the put option is "at-the-money". If you tried to sell the option, you would receive nothing for it. You already paid 3 for the option.

If you let the options expire worthless, the transaction looks like this:

Transaction	Result
Buy one GE October 100 put (price 3)	-300.00
GE October 100 put expires worthless	0.00
Net Profit or Loss	**-300.00**

How about if GE was at 110? You could exercise your right to put the asset to the option seller. But why would you? If you bought GE at 110, your right would be to sell it at 100. And why would anyone buy anything at 110, only to sell it at 100? It automatically locks in a loss of -10. Because you have the right and are not obliged to do this, the option is worthless. You paid 3 for the option.

If you let the options expire worthless, the transaction looks like this:

Transaction	Result
Buy one GE October 100 put (price 3)	-300.00
GE October 100 put expires worthless	0.00
Net Profit or Loss	**-300.00**

Finally, what happens if GE shares go to 120? Your right is to sell GE at 100. But GE shares are trading at 120. So you would have to pay 120, only to sell the shares at 100, thus locking in a loss of -20. Because you have the right and are not obliged to do this, the option is worthless. You paid 3 for the option.

The net result is the same as it would be if GE shares were at *any* price above 100. If you let the options expire worthless, the transaction looks like this:

Transaction	Result
Buy one GE October 100 put (price 3)	-300.00
GE October 100 put expires worthless	0.00
Net Profit or Loss	**-300.00**

Here is a plot of the put's profit and loss:

Figure 7

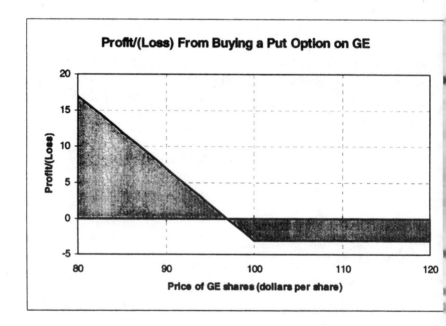

Remember, the option starts gaining value once GE shares start falling below 100. But notice how the line does not cross the zero mark until the price of GE reaches 97. This is the option purchase's breakeven. In other words, if GE finishes above 97, you lose. That's because the option does not gain enough value to overcome the purchase price. If it finishes below 97, you will earn a profit.

Notice that the breakeven price of the put is equal to the option's strike price (100) minus the price of the option when purchased (3) [100 - 3 = 97]. This is a very simple rule of thumb for calculating the breakeven of a put purchase. The breakeven of a put purchase is equal to the option's strike price minus the price of the option.

Here are the important characteristics of put buying:

1. Small cash outlay - Compared to short selling the asset, the cost of a put is much, much smaller.

2. Bearish bias - The underlying asset *must* drop in order for you to make money.

3. Limited risk - If you're wrong and the underlying asset gains value, your maximum loss potential is limited to the purchase price of the option.

4. Unlimited profit potential - If you're right about direction, the profit potential is virtually unlimited. The percentage profit available is much larger than the risk potential.

5. Poor probability - As indicated at the beginning of the report, most traders find it almost impossible to accurately guess direction consistently. When you purchase an option, you not only have to be right about market direction, your forecast must take place during a limited amount of time (prior to option expiration). In other words, you *must* guess direction accurately and your forecast *has* to take place quickly.

Review

We're rapidly progressing toward our goal, which is to grasp a basic understanding of options, and how they can be used to put the probabilities in our favor. Here's what we've learned so far:

1. A call option gives the option buyer the right to buy an underlying asset at a predetermined price. Because of this, when an underlying asset rises in price, the call option holder can buy the asset at a lower price (the predetermined exercise price from when the option was purchased), and immediately sell it at a higher price (the current open market price which is now higher). This gives the call owner the ability to buy low and sell high, thus giving them the ability to earn a profit.

2. A put option gives the option buyer the right to sell an underlying asset at a predetermined price. Because of this, when an underlying asset drops in price, the put holder can buy the asset in the open market at the current price (which is now lower), and immediately sell it at a higher price (the predetermined exercise price from when the option was purchased). This gives the put owner the ability to buy low and sell high, thus giving them the ability to earn a profit.

3. Whenever we buy something, we have to give the seller money, so money is debited from our account.

4. Whenever we sell, we receive money from a buyer, so money is credited to our account.

5. After buying something, we can sell it (via an offsetting transaction) in order to realize a profit or loss.

6. Selling short allows an investor to sell something that they don't already own. By selling an asset now, they hope that the price will drop so that they can buy back the asset at a lower price. This gives the short seller the ability to buy low and sell high, thus giving them the ability to earn a profit — only the process is reversed. The short seller sells high first, and then buys low.

7. The breakeven at expiration of a call option is equal to the strike price plus the price of the option.

8. The breakeven at expiration of a put option is equal to the strike price minus the price of the option.

9. Buying an option offers unlimited profit potential with limited risk.

10. When you buy an option, the odds of success are against you.

Calculating Profit and Loss Potential on an Option Short Sale
Part I — Selling a Call

In the previous chapters, we've learned what an option is and how profits and losses from option purchases are generated. Prior to that, we learned how a trader can sell short and make money as an asset drops in price.

The next two chapters are going to combine both concepts — options with short selling. That is, we're going to sell an option short at the inception of the trade. We will then close out the position by buying the option back in an offsetting transaction.

We'll also show you how this automatically puts the probabilities in your favor! First, we're going to show you what happens when you sell a call option short. In the next chapter we're going to sell a put option short.

It is very important to note that when you sell an option short, the buyer has all the rights. You, the option seller, have none. The option seller only has obligations.

When you sell a call option short, you are expecting the underlying asset to remain stable or decline in value. Here's why. When you sell a call, you are *not* selling short the underlying asset itself – you *are* selling short a call option. Remember that calls *increase* in value as the underlying asset increases in price. Calls *drop* in value as the underlying asset's price declines. Because we're selling short a call, we want the value of the call option to drop. Because a call's value drops when the underlying asset's price drops, we want the asset to drop in price!

Let's take a look at our example of GE (the one where we expect GE shares to drop) to see how we can determine our profit and loss potential from the short sale of a call option.

Recall in our bearish example that it's September. You know that the stock market has shown an extremely powerful seasonal tendency to drop during September and October. Because GE shares tend to rise and fall with the market, you want to implement a strategy that makes money when the market falls. You want to sell a call option.

GE is trading at 100 in September. Just as you would when you sell anything, you receive money when you sell an option. In this instance, when you sell a call, you receive money from the call option buyer. Whenever you receive money, you give the payer something, usually a service or a product. In this instance, you are giving the call option buyer a *right*. The right you are giving the call buyer is the right to buy GE shares from you at a preset price during a fixed time period. The option you sell is an October 105 call; the price of the call is 3.

The strike price of the option is 105. That means that the option buyer has the right to buy from you GE shares at 105, no matter how high or how low GE shares are. The October date means that the options expire in October (stock options and stock index options expire on the third Friday of the month). As the seller, you have received compensation from the buyer. The compensation you receive (e.g., the price of the option) is called the option premium. The price of the option in September is 3.

Now let's fast forward to October. Let's look at what the option will be worth as GE shares fluctuate. Remember, the October call option with a strike price of 105 gives the option buyer the right to buy GE shares from you at a price of 105 before October 18. Therefore, as a seller of a call option, you have the obligation to sell someone GE shares at a price of 105, no matter how high or how low the stock price actually is at the time the option is exercised.

If GE shares are trading at 80 on the New York Stock Exchange, would the option buyer want to exercise their right, call away the stock and pay 105? Of course not. Why would someone want to pay 105 when the open market price of GE is 80? Therefore, when GE shares are at 80, the option has no "exercise" value. In this case, it would be worthless at expiration. You, the option seller, could buy back the option you sold at a price of zero, but that would generate an unnecessary commission. A more likely scenario would be for you, the option seller, *and* the option buyer to just let the call expire.

If the options expired worthless, the transaction, from your perspective, would look like this:

Transaction	*Result*
Sell one GE October 105 call (price 3)	+300.00
One GE October 105 call expires worthless	0.00
Net Profit or Loss	**+300.00**

How about if GE is trading at 90? Same thing. No trader would want to pay 105 (as would be the call buyer's right) if they could buy GE in the open market at 90. Therefore, when GE shares are at 90, the option has no "exercise" value. In this case, it would be worthless at expiration. As the person who sold the call option short, you could buy it back for zero, but that would generate an unnecessary commission. A more likely scenario would be for you, the option seller, *and* the option buyer to just let the call expire.

If the options expired worthless, the transaction, from your perspective, would look like this:

Transaction	Result
Sell one GE October 105 call (price 3)	+300.00
One GE October 105 call expires worthless	0.00
Net Profit or Loss	**+300.00**

In both instances, there is no value in exercising the option. The same thing is true if GE shares were at 100.

But what if GE shares were at the strike price — 105? In this case, it really doesn't matter. The option buyer could either buy the shares in the open market for 105, or exercise the option and buy GE shares from you at 105. If the option buyer exercised his right to buy GE shares from you, you would simply buy the stock in the open market for 105 and sell the shares to the call buyer for 105. You, however, have previously been paid for the option that you sold. In the stock portion of this transaction, you are simply buying at one price (105, the open market price) and then immediately selling the stock at the same price (105, the option's exercise price). Since there is no added value to exercising the option, it is essentially worthless. Again, as the person who sold the call option short, you could buy it back for zero, but that would generate an unnecessary commission. A more likely scenario would be for you, the option seller, and the option buyer to just let the call expire.

If the options expired worthless, the transaction from your perspective would look like this:

Transaction	Result
Sell one GE October 105 call (price 3)	+300.00
One GE October 105 call expires worthless	0.00
Net Profit or Loss	**+300.00**

If you buy back the option for nothing, the transaction looks like this:

Transaction	Result
Sell one GE October 105 call (price 3)	+300.00
Buy back one GE October 105 call (price 0)	0.00
Net Profit or Loss	**+300.00**

If the call option buyer happened to exercise his option to buy, the transaction would look like this from your perspective:

Transaction	Result
Sell one GE October 105 call (price 3)	+300.00
Buy 100 shares of GE at 105	-10,500.00
Sell 100 shares of GE at 105	+10,500.00
Net Profit or Loss	**+300.00**

How about when GE is at 110? At 110, the options have value. The option buyer could exercise his right to "call" away the stock from you and buy it at 105. This forces you to deliver the stock. If the stock is at 110, you would have to buy the stock in the open market at 110 and sell it at 105, the exercise price of the option. In this instance, you lose -5 from the exercise, but you've already collected 3, so your net loss is -2. Also, as we showed, you could simply offset the transaction by buying the option. If you bought the option for its exercise value (5), it would show up on your account as a debit, or as a minus.

If you held the call option until the option buyer exercised it, the transaction would look like this:

Transaction	*Result*
Sell one GE October 105 call (price 3)	+300.00
Buy 100 shares of GE at 110	-11,000.00
Sell 100 shares of GE at 105	+10,500.00
Net Profit or Loss	**-200.00**

If you bought back the call option in an offsetting transaction, it would look like this:

Transaction	*Result*
Sell one GE October 105 call (price 3)	+300.00
Buy back one GE October 105 call (price 5)	-500.00
Net Profit or Loss	**-200.00**

Finally, what happens if GE shares go to 120? Again, the option buyer could exercise his right to "call" away and buy the shares at 105. This would force you to buy the stock in the open market at 120, then sell the shares you just bought for 120 to the option buyer at the exercise price of 105. In this instance, you lose -15 from the exercise, but you've already collected 3, so your loss is -12. Also, as we showed, you could simply offset the transaction by buying the option. If you bought the option for its exercise value (15), it would show up on your account as a debit, or as a minus.

If you held the call option until the option buyer exercised it, the transaction would look like this:

Transaction	*Result*
Sell one GE October 105 call (price 3)	+300.00
Buy 100 shares of GE at 120	-12,000.00
Sell 100 shares of GE at 105	+10,500.00
Net Profit or Loss	**-1,200.00**

If you bought back the call option in an offsetting transaction, it would look like this:

Transaction	Result
Sell one GE October 105 call (price 3)	+300.00
Buy back one GE October 105 call (price 15)	-1,500.00
Net Profit or Loss	**-1,200.00**

Here's a graph of the call short sale's profit and loss:

Figure 8

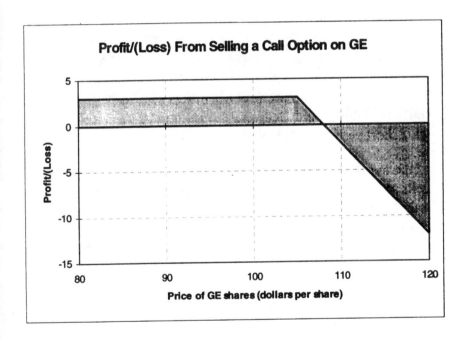

This graph is critical to understanding why the odds are in your favor when you sell an option. Remember, GE shares are trading at a price of 100. Notice that the place in which the profit/loss line drops below zero (the breakeven) is somewhere between 100 and 110. The exact price is 108 – the price of the option when you sold it, plus the strike price. As long as GE shares stay below 108, you make money. If GE shares are above 108 at expiration, the option seller loses. This is the same breakeven as the option buyer, only the option buyer wins if GE goes above 108 and loses if they are below 108 at expiration.

Notice that, if you are bearish, and the stock goes down, you make money. If you are bearish and the stock stands still, staying at 100, you still make money. If you are bearish and the stock *goes up* 5% to 105, you *still* make money. It is the location of the breakeven which is crucial to explaining why option selling has such a high probability of success. For the option seller to lose, GE shares have to rise more than 8% in less than two months (from early-September to mid-October)!! A rise of that magnitude over such a short period simply doesn't happen very often.

That means the odds of GE shares being below 108 in about 6 weeks are going to be extremely high. Consequently, because there are three possible ways in which the call option seller makes money (if GE drops any amount, if GE stands still, and if GE rises less than 8% during a six-week period) the option *seller's* odds of success are extremely high. On the other hand, the option *buyer's* odds of success are very low, as they win in only one scenario, an extremely large move upward in GE share's price.

However, as the word suggests, an *extreme* move is highly improbable. So the odds of suffering a loss are remote. Thus, the probability is high, but so is the risk potential.

Characteristics of call selling:

1. Small cash outlay - Compared to selling the asset short, the margin requirements are reduced.

2. Slight bearish bias - The underlying asset can stand still or decline in price for you to make money.

3. Unlimited risk - If you're wrong and the underlying asset increases in value, your risk is as large as if you were selling short the asset.

4. Limited profit potential - If you're right about direction, the profit potential is limited to the premium you receive when you sell the call.

5. High probability of profit - Selling a call option *automatically* puts the odds in your favor. By selling a call, the asset can drop in price, stand still, or even go up a little, and you'll still make money. The only situation in which you can lose is if the asset goes up in price by a substantial amount.

<u>Calculating Profit and Loss Potential on an Option Short Sale Part II — Selling a Put</u>

In the world of elementary school arithmetic, we all learned that when you multiplied a negative number by another negative number, the resulting product was a positive number.

This concept has a loose link to the final strategy we're going to look at, because we're going to combine short selling (a strategy that we showed makes money in a *negative* market environment) with a put option (which we showed increases in value in a *negative* market environment) to come up with an overall option strategy that makes money in a *positive* market environment!

That is, we're going to combine two negatives to create a positive.

What we're going to do is sell short a put option. When you sell short a put, you make money if the underlying asset *increases* in value or if it stands still. Here's why:

Remember that when you sell short, you make money if the "thing" you've sold short declines in price. That's because if the "thing" drops in price, you can buy it back for less than what you sold it for. That is, you've bought low and sold high. Only you bought and sold in reverse, selling high first and *then* buying low.

It is critically important that you realize what it is we're selling short when we sell a put. You are *not* selling short the underlying asset itself – you *are* selling short a put. Remember that puts *increase* in value as the underlying asset declines in price. Puts *drop* in value as the underlying asset's price rises. Because we're selling short a put, we want the value of the put to drop. Because a put's value drops when the underlying asset's price rises, we want the asset to rise in price! A few examples will obviously help.

Remember, whenever we buy something, we have to give the seller money, so money is debited from our account. When we sell, we receive money from a buyer, so money is credited to our account. After selling an option, it can either expire worthless, the option buyer can exercise his right, or it can be "bought back" in an offsetting transaction.

Let's look at stock PQR, which is trading at 100 in December. You are bullish on PQR. You expect the stock to rise in price. That means you expect the put options to *drop* in price. You decide to sell short a January at-the-money put. At-the-money means that the option's strike price and the stock's current price are the same. That means the option's strike price must be 100. January corresponds to the option's expiration date.

By selling a put, you are giving someone the right to sell PQR shares if they drop in value, so you sell them a put option with a strike price of 100 and an expiration date of January 19 (stock options and stock index options expire on the third Friday of every month). Remember, the strike price is the price at which the option can be exercised. This means that the buyer will have the right to sell PQR shares to you for 100 before the January options expire on January 19, no matter how high or how low PQR shares are.

As the seller of the option, you will be obliged to buy PQR shares if the buyer of the option exercises his right. You require compensation for taking on that obligation. The compensation you require (e.g. the price of the option) is called the option premium. The price of the option in December is 6.

Now let's fast forward to January. Let's look at what the option will be worth as PQR shares fluctuate. Remember, the January put option with a strike price of 100 gives the buyer the right but not the obligation to sell to you PQR shares at 100 before January 19.

If PQR shares are trading at 80 on the New York Stock Exchange, here's what would happen. The option buyer would have the right to sell the stock to you at a price of 100. Remember, **the person who sells the put option has the obligation to buy the asset at the preset price.** Therefore, the option buyer could buy the stock in the open market at 80 and immediately sell it to the option grantor at 100. You, the option seller, would have to buy the stock at 100. You could then do one of two things: hang on to the stock, or, more likely, sell it in the open market where PQR shares are trading at 80.

If you hold the option you sold short until it was exercised, the transaction would look like this (Remember, you sold the option for 6. Stock options are worth $100 per point):

Transaction	Result
Sell one PQR January 100 put (price 6)	+600.00
Buy 100 shares of PQR at 100 when the option is exercised	-10,000.00
Sell 100 shares of PQR at 80	+8,000.00
Net Profit or Loss	**-1,400.00**

If you choose to offset the short sale of the put by buying it back for its exercise value of 20 (the exercise value is 20 because that is how much the option buyer would get if he or she exercised their right), the transaction looks like this:

Transaction	Result
Sell one PQR January 100 put (price 6)	+600.00
Buy one PQR January 100 put (price 20)	-2,000.00
Net Profit or Loss	**-1,400.00**

What about when PQR is at 90? The option buyer could exercise the option, buy the stock in the open market at 90, then sell it to you for 100. You would have to buy the stock at 100. Like before, you could then do one of two things: hang on to the stock, or more likely sell it in the open market, in which PQR shares are trading at 90.

If you hold the option you sold short until it was exercised, the transaction would look like this (Remember, you sold the option for 6. Stock options are worth $100 per point):

Transaction	Result
Sell one PQR January 100 put (price 6)	+600.00
Buy 100 shares of PQR at 100 when the option is exercised	-10,000.00
Sell 100 shares of PQR at 90	+9,000.00
Net Profit or Loss	-400.00

If you choose to offset the short sale of the put by buying it back for its exercise value of 10, the transaction looks like this:

Transaction	Result
Sell one PQR January 100 put (price 6)	+600.00
Buy one PQR January 100 put (price 10)	-1,000.00
Net Profit or Loss	-400.00

How about if PQR is trading at 100? In this case, it really doesn't matter. If the option buyer exercised his option to put PQR in your hands, you'd have to buy it at 100. But you could immediately sell it for 100. So you wouldn't have a profit or a loss on the exercise; it would merely be a breakeven transaction. Thus, there is no added value to exercising the option, so it is essentially worthless. In this case, the put option is "at-the-money". If you bought back the option, you would pay a commission, but nothing else. You already received 6 for the option when you sold it short.

Transaction	Result
Sell one PQR January 100 put (price 6)	+600.00
Buy 100 shares of PQR at 100 when the option is exercised	-10,000.00
Sell 100 shares of PQR at 100	+10,000.00
Net Profit or Loss	**+600.00**

If you choose to offset the short sale of the put by buying it back for its exercise value of 0, the transaction looks like this:

Transaction	Result
Sell one PQR January 100 put (price 6)	+600.00
Buy one PQR January 100 put (price 0)	0.00
Net Profit or Loss	**+600.00**

If you let the options expire worthless, the transaction looks like this:

Transaction	Result
Sell one PQR January 100 put (price 6)	+600.00
PQR January 100 put expires worthless	0.00
Net Profit or Loss	**+600.00**

How about if PQR was at 110? The put buyer could exercise his right to put the stock to you at 100. But why would he? No one would ever willingly buy PQR at 110, only to sell it to you for 100. It automatically locks in a loss of -10 for him. Because he has the right but is not obliged to do this, he would just do nothing, so the option is worthless. You sold the option for 6.

If the options expire worthless, the transaction looks like this:

Transaction	Result
Sell one PQR January 100 put (price 6)	+600.00
PQR January 100 put expires worthless	0.00
Net Profit or Loss	**+600.00**

Finally, what happens if PQR shares go to 120? The put option buyer's right is to sell PQR at 100. But PQR shares are trading at 120. So he would have to pay 120, only to sell the shares at 100, thus locking in a loss of -20. Because selling is his right and not his obligation, he does nothing. Therefore, the option is worthless. You received 6 for the option.

The net result is the same as it would be if PQR shares were at any price above 100. If the options expire worthless, the transaction looks like this:

Transaction	Result
Sell one PQR January 100 put (price 6)	+600.00
PQR January 100 put expires worthless	0.00
Net Profit or Loss	**+600.00**

Here is a profit/loss graph showing the results from selling the put option on PQR shares:

Figure 9

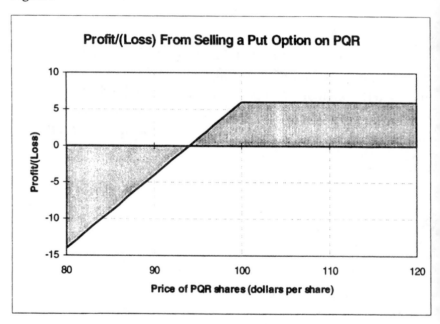

As with the graph associated with selling a call, this graph is critical to understanding why the odds are in the put seller's favor. Remember, PQR shares are trading at a price of 100. Notice that the place in which the profit/loss line drops below zero (the breakeven) is somewhere between 90 and 95. The exact price is 94 – the price of the option when you sold it, minus the strike price. As long as PQR shares stay above 94, you make money. If PQR shares are above 94 at expiration, the option seller wins. This is the same breakeven point as for the put option buyer, only the option buyer wins if PQR shares are below 94. The option buyer loses if the shares are above 94 at expiration.

Notice that, if you are bullish, and the stock goes up, you make money. If you are bullish and the stock stands still, staying at 100, you still make money. If you are bullish and you are wrong, and the stock goes down 5% to 95, you *still* make money. It is the location of the breakeven which is crucial to explaining why option selling has such a high probability of success. For the option seller to lose, PQR shares have to drop more than 6% in a little more than a month! For most stocks, a drop of that magnitude over such a short period simply doesn't happen very often.

That means the odds of PQR shares being above 94 in about 5 weeks are going to be extremely high. Consequently, because there are three possible ways in which the put option seller makes money (if PQR rises any amount, if PQR stands still, and if PQR drops by less than 6% during a five-week period) the option *seller's* odds of success are extremely high. On the other hand, the option *buyer's* odds of success are very low, as he wins in only one scenario, an extremely large move downward in PQR's share price.

Characteristics of put selling:

1. Small cash outlay - Compared to buying the asset itself, the margin requirements are much smaller.

2. Slight bullish bias - The underlying asset can stand still or rise in price for you to make money.

3. Unlimited risk - If you're wrong and the underlying asset drops in price, your risk is as large as if you were buying the asset itself.

4. Limited profit potential - If you're right about direction, the profit potential is limited to the premium you receive when you sell the put option.

5. High probability of profit - Selling a put option automatically puts the odds in your favor. By selling a put, the asset can rise in price, stand still, or even go down a little, and you'll still make money. The only situation in which you can lose is if the asset goes down in price a lot.

Putting The Pieces Together

Here's what we've learned in this book, so far:

1. A call option gives the option buyer the right to buy an underlying asset at a predetermined price. Because of this, when an underlying asset rises in price, the call option holder can buy the asset at a lower price (the predetermined exercise price established at the time the option was purchased), and immediately sell it at a higher price (the current open market price which is now higher). This gives the call owner the ability to buy low and sell high, thus giving him the ability to earn a profit.

2. A put option gives the option buyer the right to sell an underlying asset at a predetermined price. Because of this, when an underlying asset drops in price, the put holder can buy the asset in the open market at the current price (which is now lower), and immediately sell it at a higher price (the predetermined exercise price established at the time the option was purchased). This gives the put owner the ability to buy low and sell high, thus giving him the ability to earn a profit.

3. Whenever we buy something, we have to give the seller money, so money is debited from our account.

4. Whenever we sell, we receive money from a buyer, so money is credited to our account.

5. After buying something, we can sell it (via an offsetting transaction) in order to realize a profit or loss.

6. Selling short allows an investor to sell something that he

doesn't already own. **By selling an asset now, he hopes that** the price will drop so that he can buy back the asset at a lower price. This gives the short seller the ability to buy low and sell high, thus giving him the ability to earn a profit — only the process is reversed. The short seller sells high first, and then buys low.

7. The breakeven at expiration of a call option is equal to the strike price plus the price of the option.

8. The breakeven at expiration of a put option is equal to the strike price minus the price of the option.

9. Buying an option offers unlimited profit potential with limited risk.

10. When you buy an option, the odds of success are against you.

11. When you sell an option, the odds are automatically in your favor.

12. The seller of an option has potentially unlimited risk.

13. Small cash outlay - Compared to trading the underlying asset itself, the margin requirements for trading options are much smaller.

While we've taken an important first step in the learning process, it is just that – *a first step*. There are many more aspects to option trading that one must learn before he or she begins actual trading. It is beyond the scope of this book to cover them all, but the next chapter will introduce those to you.

<u>Taking It To The Next Level</u>

What you've learned so far is sufficient to get started. There is, however, additional information that you could gather to improve your success to the next realm.

For example, we discussed how one could buy a call or a put to limit risk while allowing for potentially unlimited profits. The bad news is that the odds are *automatically* against you. We also discussed at length how you could sell a call or a put to instantly put the odds in your favor. But that would leave the investor exposed to potentially unlimited risk. The good news is that there are simple solutions.

One method for limiting risk while putting the odds in your favor is using a contingency order. Using our PQR put sale as an example, let's say that if PQR shares (now at 100) dropped to 90, we would exit the option position in an offsetting transaction. In that instance, our loss would be limited. The problem is, what if PQR shares gapped lower, let's say from 91 to 70. Although this is extremely unlikely, it is certainly possible. Such an occurrence would be devastating, and unpreventable.

A *better* solution would be to use a spread. By combining option purchases and short sales, you can create an option spread that both limits risk and puts the probability of profit in your favor. This is *exactly* the strategy I used to come up with 306 trades during a three-year period, with only 5 losers. That's right, using a simple spread, I discovered 306 **<u>limited risk</u>** option trades, of which only 5 lost. I didn't have to worry about any "gap" moves in the underlying asset. I didn't have any sleepless nights. I simply implemented a limited-risk option strategy designed to win at least 90% of the time, and that was it.

The strategy I used is called a credit spread, because I was paid to implement the spread. A credit spread is a strategy where you sell an option and then simultaneously buy an option that is further out-of-the-money. For example, let's say you are a stock index trader. The index you are following is trading at 400. If you were bullish, you would sell a 380 put and buy a 375 put. As long as the index stayed above 380, you'd win. In other words, if the index went up, you'd make money. If the index stood still, you'd make money. If the index dropped by 5%, you'd make money. Only if the index dropped by more than 5% would you lose. That's why the odds are so fantastic – there is only one situation that's a loser, and even then, the loss is limited*.

You can also implement a credit spread that has a bearish bias. In this instance, you might sell the 420 call and simultaneously buy the 425 call. In this instance, if the index dropped, you'd make money. If the market stood still, you'd make money. If the index rallied 5%, you'd still make money. Only if the index rallied by more than 5% would you lose. As it is with selling a put credit spread, the odds are fantastic because there is only one situation in which you lose, and even then, the loss potential is completely limited.

What's really special is combining a call credit spread and a put credit spread. Remember early on we showed that the stock market rarely trades up or down more than 5% in a month. You can put that phenomenon to work for you by using options. By simply selling a call credit spread and a put credit spread at the same time, you can earn income while the market trades up and down in a very wide range. History shows us that this type of

---

* - As I mentioned earlier, there seems to be an exception to nearly everything in trading. In this instance, cash-settled, American-style index options *can* behave unusually if they go "deep-in-the-money" as expiration approaches. Please be sure to read *Characteristics and Risks of Standardized Options* before trading.

strategy should make money at least 90% of the time.

My actual results show that in the right market, <u>even better</u> results can be achieved.

Results like this come from using just one type of spread. There are virtually an *unlimited* number of strategies and option combinations you can utilize to make money and control risk.

That leads up to the next aspect of trading, putting the odds in your favor. Remember in Chapter 3 **Putting The Probabilities On Your Side** we showed that you could look at past market activity, and analyze a market's tendency to trade within a range, to derive a probability of profit. There is actually a much better, more reliable method for calculating probability - one that will let you instantly spot a trade with a 70%, 80%, even 90% probability of profit.

We introduce this concept in our highly-acclaimed video *ODDS - The Key to 90% Winners*. For example, let's say you were looking at selling the GE September 100 put. We stated that the ODDS were in your favor when you sold an option. Did you know that the precise probability of profit for that trade is 64.78%?

Recall that we stated in an earlier chapter, **Understanding Option Terminology**, that one of the factors impacting an option's value is risk and reward of the underlying asset (i.e., its volatility). We can use volatility[5] to precisely calculate the probability of profit using advanced algebra and volatility. We can also *reverse the process* to come up with a trade based on our desired probability of profit.

[5] Volatility is not that hard to find. If you don't already have software that calculates volatility for you, there are a wide array of resources that can provide that volatility number for you. There are publications that provide volatility data for stocks and commodities, inexpensive software products, plus, in our video, we even show you one method for calculating volatility yourself on a hand held calculator.

Using these formulas (which are quite simple once you've gotten the hang of it), one can easily spot trades with a 90% chance of winning, in just a matter of moments!!

For example, in mid December 1994, the market was tumbling. Everywhere you looked there was an incredible level of fear. Mexico had just devalued its peso and was on the verge of collapse. The situation caused a currency crisis in this country and threatened to take down several big U.S. banks. At the same time, the country's largest mutual fund had just revealed it made a massive $1+ billion accounting goof that resulted in a suspension of a distribution to shareholders. And at the same time that all this was going on, the extent of the debacle in derivatives was starting to be realized by investors worldwide. Nick Leeson at Barings Bank had been blown out of the water, torpedoing a centuries old financial institution. Meanwhile, the horror of billion dollar losses in Orange County was being made public, with certain bankruptcy an unfortunate consequence.

While all of this was going on Fed Chairman Alan Greenspan testified before Congress and said that the economy was still very strong and that wholesale inflation was likely to pass through to the consumer. Bonds tanked on his comments.

In the middle of all this, I thought gloom was too pervasive. I wanted to try a bullish trade. *But I wanted my trade to have an overwhelming chance of success.* I wanted to find a bullish trade that had at least a 90% chance of success.

Fortunately, there was (and is) an easy solution. Using mathematical equations I developed from the option pricing models, you can input readily available financial information to instantly come up with option trades that have a 90% chance of success.

Using these equations, I did just that – I looked for a trade with a 90% chance of winning. The exact probability of profit of the trade I found was 87.6% and it earned nearly $2,750.00 in just seven days!

The final, and perhaps the most important, aspect of all is determining how much to invest in a trade. If you've ever read about the big money makers, like George Soros and Paul Tudor Jones, or if you've read the book *Market Wizards*, you know that this factor is the most important part of their decision-making process.

Amazingly, this happens to be *the* most overlooked aspect to trading. Think about it. When you watch an analyst on TV, he tells you that he likes a stock, but he doesn't tell you how much to buy.

If you purchase a book that reveals market forecasting methods designed to pick tops and bottoms accurately, you're still only part of the way there. That's because not every signal is accurate. So if you invest too much in the wrong signals and not enough in the right signals, you could still end up losing money! Investing the same dollar amount in every trade is one solution, but what if that dollar amount is the wrong amount?

Unfortunately, software trading systems fail miserably when it comes to this. You see, when you use "system" software, it tells you when to buy and sell. But does it tell you how many contracts to buy? No way, because it can't!

Given this information, if determining the right amount to invest is the single most crucial factor in trading, and there are no option trading sources out there that can help with this critical success factor, is it any wonder that there are so few millionaire option traders?!

Again, there are solutions, even to this puzzle. There *is* an interesting, yet simple, formula that uses risk and reward analysis, along with probability of profit, to tell you how much of your portfolio to invest in a trade. The answer to the formula is the precise portfolio allocation that will literally let you maximize your profit potential while minimizing your risk. The key element in this is, of course probability, and that's where probability analysis can be vital.

Putting all of this together – risk, reward and probability – won't be super easy, but it *will* be well worth it. That's because once you've mastered these techniques (which will come naturally as you become more familiar with options) you will be able to instantly spot a limited risk, high probability option trade, and invest the precise amount so that your profits are maximized and your risk is completely limited and in control.

In other words, once you understand how to calculate risk, reward (which you learned in this book) and probability, you'll be able to spot a trade that has an almost certain chance at being correct. The trade will have completely limited risk. And you'll be able to know precisely how much to invest so that your reward potential is at the highest level possible, while maintaining a safe cushion. Best of all, this process will be totally automatic, so that it will take you only 30 seconds.

SPECIAL MESSAGE FROM DON FISHBACK

Buyers of OPTIONS FOR BEGINNERS, are entitled to a free Special Report. The Report is called "*HOW TO WIN 80% OF YOUR TRADES OR BETTER*".

If you did not receive your copy, please call my office and tell them that you want your free report. That number is:

1-859-224-4424

1-859-224-4452 (fax)

Or Write: Don Fishback
1040 Monarch Street, Suite 110
Lexington, KY 40513